Planet Earth

Copyright © Kingfisher Publications Plc 2006
KINGFISHER
Published in the United States by Kingfisher, an imprint of Henry Holt and Company LLC,
175 Fifth Avenue, New York, New York 10010. First published in Great Britain by Kingfisher Publications plc,
an imprint of Macmillan Children's Books, London.

Distributed in Canada by H. B. Fenn and Company Ltd.

Library of Congress Cataloging-in-Publication Data has been applied for.

ISBN: 978-0-7534-6179-2

Kingfisher books are available for special promotions and premiums.
For details contact: Director of Special Markets, Holtzbrinck Publishers.

Printed in China
10 9 8 7 6 5 4 3 2 1
1TR/0608/PROSP/RNBW/140MA/F

Acknowledgments
The publishers would like to thank the following for permission to reproduce their material. Every care has been taken
to trace copyright holders. However, if there have been unintentional omissions or failure to trace copyright holders,
we apologize and will, if informed, endeavor to make corrections in any future edition.
b = bottom, c = center, l = left, t = top, r = right

Photographs: *cover* 1 Photolibrary.com; 2-3 Photolibrary.com; 4-5 Corbis Clay Perry; 6 Getty Imagebank; 7 Getty Stone; 8*bl*
Photolibrary.com; 8-9 Science Photo Library Roger Harris; 9*b* Photolibrary.com; 12*l* Corbis Rupak de Chowdhuri; 13*t* Photolibrary.com; 13*br*
Getty Photodisc; 12-13 Science Photo Library Pekka Parvianen; 16-17 Getty Imagebank; 16*cr* Photolibrary.com; 18*bl* Corbis NASA; 18-19
Getty Stone; 20-21 Corbis Tom Bean; 21*br* Getty AFP Yoshikazu Tsuno; 22-21 Corbis R. T. Holcomb; 23*tr* Corbis Charles & Josette Lenars;
24-25 Photolibrary.com; 24*c* Corbis Galen Rowell; 25*tl* Getty Stone; 26*l* Corbis Michael Freeman; 26-27 Getty Imagebank; 27*t*
Photolibrary.com; 29 Corbis Audrey Gibson; 30-31 Getty Imagebank; 30*b* Corbis Robert Weight; 31*tr* Arcticphoto; 32-33 Corbis Yann
Arthus-Bertrand; 32*bl* Frank Lane Picture Agency Minden Pictures; 33*tl* Photolibrary.com; 34-35 Photolibrary.com; 34*tr* Frank Lane Picture
Agency Minden Pictures; 34*b* Getty Taxi; 35*bl* Corbis Craig Tuttle; 36-37 Frank Lane Picture Agency Minden Pictures; 36*b* Getty Stone; 37*tr*
Corbis Michael Yamashita; 38-39 Getty Digital Vision; 38*b* Getty Photodisc; 39*br* Corbis Tim Wright; 40-41 Getty Digital Vision; 40*bl* Getty
Photodisc; 41*c* Getty Photodisc; 48 Alamy Bryan & Cherry Alexander

Commissioned photography on pages 42–47 by Andy Crawford
Project maker and photo shoot coordinator: Jo Connor
Thank you to models Alex Bandy, Alastair Carter, Tyler Gunning, and Lauren Signist.

SCIENCE KIDS

Planet Earth

Deborah Chancellor

KINGFISHER
NEW YORK

Contents

What is Earth?

Earth is a planet in space. It is one of eight large planets that circle around the Sun in our solar system. Seen from space, Earth looks blue. This is because most of it is covered with oceans and seas.

Central America

The continents

The large areas of land are called continents. We can see the shape of the continents in photos taken from space. This large continent is South America.

South America

The atmosphere

There is a blanket of gases around Earth called the atmosphere. White clouds swirl around in our planet's atmosphere.

solar system—*the planets that revolve around the Sun*

atmosphere

gases—*shapeless substances that can fill any space*

Inside Earth

Earth is a rocky planet. It is divided into three main parts—the crust, the mantle, and the core. We live on the crust, which is a thin layer of solid rock. Not far below our feet, the rock is so hot that it is liquid.

crust

The crust

In some places under the sea Earth's crust is only 3.7 mi. (6km) thick. Under most of the land the crust is around 22 mi. (35km) thick.

solid rock—*cool, hard rock*

The core

The core is the hottest part of Earth. At the core temperatures can reach up to 9,032°F (5,000°C).

mantle

inner core

outer core

The mantle

The hot rock in Earth's mantle melts and becomes liquid. We can see molten rock when a volcano erupts.

molten rock—hot, liquid rock

The water cycle

The world's water is never used up. The Sun warms up seawater, turning it into water vapor. This vapor rises into the air and then falls as rain. The rain then flows back to the sea. This is called the water cycle.

Sun heats seawater, making water vapor

Water falls as rain

Water world

Most of the world's water is in the oceans. Only one percent of all of the world's water moves around in the water cycle.

vapor—water in the air

Water falls
as rain

Water vapor
rises to form
clouds

Water collects
in rivers and
flows to the sea

Rain

Water vapor in clouds falls to the ground as rain. Some places get a lot of rain. Mawsynram, in northern India, gets more than 36 ft. (11m) of rain every year. It is the wettest place in the world.

Weather and climate

Weather happens when the air around us changes. Air can be moving or still, hot or cold, wet or dry, or a mixture of these things. Water has a big part to play in the weather. Without it, there would be no clouds, rain, or fog.

Tropical climate
The weather that a place usually experiences over a long period of time is called its climate. Climates vary in different parts of the world. In tropical places the climate is hot and steamy.

pollution—*harmful waste*

Desert climate

In deserts the climate is dry. On average, a desert gets less than one inch of rain in one year. If all of the rain falls at once, there may be floods.

Trapping heat

Pollution in the air may trap some of the Sun's heat and stop it from escaping back into space. As a result, our climate may be getting warmer every year.

tropical—*an area around the middle of Earth with very hot, dry weather*

Clouds, rain, and snow

Clouds are made up of millions of tiny water droplets or ice crystals. Water droplets in clouds join together to make raindrops, and ice crystals combine to form snowflakes. Clouds come in many different shapes and sizes.

Snow

Snowflakes usually melt on their way down to Earth. But if the air close to the ground is freezing, we get snow.

droplets—very small drops of liquid

Different clouds

Low stratus clouds can bring rain. Fluffy cumulus clouds are seen on sunny days. High, wispy cirrus clouds are made out of ice.

Cirrus cloud

Cumulus cloud

Thunderclouds

Cumulonimbus clouds are the biggest clouds of all. Some are taller than Earth's highest mountain, Mount Everest! They bring heavy rain, thunder, and lightning.

Stratus cloud

ice crystals—*tiny pieces of ice*

Wind

Wind is air that moves around. It can be as gentle as a breeze or as rough as a hurricane. Wind occurs when the Sun warms the air, making it rise upward. Cold air rushes in to fill the gap, causing the wind to blow.

When the wind blows

Wind travels at different speeds. A light breeze makes clouds drift across the sky. Stronger winds make trees sway, while very strong winds, called hurricanes, can cause a lot of damage.

Air currents

Birds can glide on rising
currents of warm air.
Seagulls hardly need to
flap their wings in order
to stay high up in the sky.

currents—*movements in the same direction*

Hurricanes and tornadoes

Hurricanes and tornadoes are dangerous windstorms. Hurricanes form over the sea, and when they reach land, they can cause terrible damage. Tornadoes are powerful whirlwinds that form over land.

Hurricane
This satellite photo shows a hurricane in the Caribbean Sea. It is heading for the coast of Florida.

satellite photo—a photograph taken from a satellite that is orbiting Earth

Twister

Tornadoes are also called twisters. The wind speed in the center of a twister reaches almost 250 mph (400km/h)—this is the fastest wind on Earth.

whirlwind—a strong wind that blows in a spiral shape

Earthquakes

Earth's crust is made of many pieces called plates. They are always sliding past or pushing up against each other. Sometimes this movement makes the ground split open, causing an earthquake.

How earthquakes happen

When two plates move suddenly, the ground trembles and shakes, and deep cracks appear on Earth's surface.

movement of plate

fault—*a break in Earth's crust*

Fault line

This huge crack in the ground is the San Andreas Fault in California. Two of Earth's plates grind past each other there. This has caused some tremendous earthquakes.

Earthquake drill

Earthquakes are common in some places. In Japan schoolchildren wear protective hats when practicing what to do if there is an earthquake.

drill—a repeated practice or exercise

Volcanoes

A volcano is a mountain made out of molten rock called lava. This molten rock comes from deep under the ground, and it forces its way up through cracks and weak points in Earth's crust. Volcanoes can form on land or deep underwater.

Inside a volcano
Molten rock, called magma, collects in a chamber. When the volcano erupts, it is forced upward through a vent.

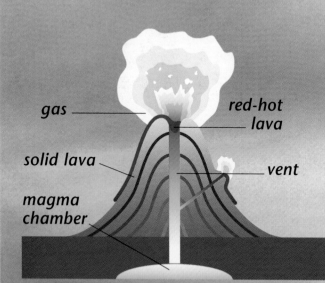

gas

red-hot lava

solid lava

vent

magma chamber

Bubbling mud

The land around volcanoes becomes very hot. Pools of mud or water bubble and boil on Earth's surface.

Giant volcano

The biggest active volcano in the world is in Hawaii. This lava flow is from the Mauna Ulu crater there.

magma—*molten rock underground*

Mountains

Mountains form over millions of years. They are made when two plates under Earth's crust push together, forcing up huge folds of rock. As the mountain is pushed upward, ice, wind, and weather wear it down. This is called erosion.

plates—large areas of land that "float" on the molten rock underneath them

The Alps

The Alps in Europe are a few million years old. Young mountains have jagged peaks. The weather has not had time to smooth down the sharp edges of rock.

The Himalayas

The 14 tallest mountains in the world are in the Himalayas in Asia. These mountains are more than 50 million years old.

peak—*the top of a mountain*

Rivers and lakes

All rivers carry water to the sea. Some are so powerful that they can change the shape of the land that they pass through. They carry rocks and mud along with them, creating deep valleys and gorges as they go.

Lakes

Lakes are large pools of water surrounded by land. They can form in volcanic craters or in valleys made by the movements of Earth's crust.

A river's journey

A river begins its journey in high ground, where it quickly flows downhill. When a river enters a valley, it flows slowly in bends, which are called meanders.

valleys—*areas of low land*

Grand Canyon

The Colorado river has carved out the deepest gorge in the world. The fast-moving waters have worn away, which has helped create the amazing Grand Canyon in northern Arizona.

gorges—*valleys with steep sides*

The oceans

Oceans cover most of planet Earth. They are deeper in some parts than in others. This is because the ocean floor is not flat. There are mountains, valleys, plains, and deep trenches under the sea.

Big blue sea

The five main oceans are the Arctic, Atlantic, Pacific, Indian and Southern. The largest of these oceans is the Pacific.

volcano

shipwreck

deep trench

trenches—long, narrow valleys

Low tide

At low tide rock pools can be found on rocky beaches. The pools are covered over again at high tide.

Islands

Some underwater mountains and volcanoes are so tall that they rise above the surface of the water. Many islands are actually the tips of underwater mountains.

mountain range

island

The poles

The North Pole is in the middle of the Arctic Ocean. This is a frozen ocean and is surrounded by the world's most northern lands. The South Pole is located in the center of the continent of Antarctica. Most of Antarctica is covered with thick ice.

Antarctic science

Antarctica is the coldest and windiest continent. The only people who live there are scientists, who work in research stations.

glaciers—moving rivers of ice

Icebergs

In Antarctica and the Arctic icebergs break away from ice sheets or glaciers and float in the icy ocean. We see only a tiny part of an iceberg—the rest is hidden underwater.

Northern Lights

The Northern Lights, or aurora borealis, can be seen in northern Canada, Alaska, and Scandinavia. This spectacular display takes place high up in the atmosphere.

Deserts

Deserts are the driest places on Earth because it hardly ever rains there. Some deserts are sandy, and others are rocky. Some are very hot, while others are freezing cold in the winter.

Desert plants

Cactus plants grow in deserts in the United States. They can live for a long time without rain because they store water in their thick stems. Some birds make their homes in cactus stems.

cactus—*a plant that can grow in places with little rain*

Wind erosion

Deserts can be windy places. Wind blasts sand at tall rocks, gradually wearing them away. The rocks in Monument Valley, in Arizona and Utah, show how wind can change the landscape in a desert.

Biggest desert

The Sahara, in northern Africa, is the largest desert in the world. It contains the world's tallest sand dunes, which are up to 1,410 ft. (430m) high and 3 mi. (5km) long.

sand dunes—*big hills of sand that are formed by the wind*

Forests

A forest is a large area of land that is covered in trees. Around one fifth of the world is covered with forests. In the past forests grew over a lot more of the planet, but people have cut down many of the trees.

Deciduous

Trees that lose their leaves in the winter are called deciduous. The leaves change color and drop from the trees in the fall.

Rainforest

Rainforests grow in hot countries where there is a lot of rain. The wettest rainforests have more than 32 ft. (10m) of rainfall per year.

Evergreen

Big forests of evergreen trees grow in northern parts of the world. Evergreen trees do not lose their leaves in the winter. Their branches slope down, so the snow slides off of them.

rainforest—a thick, tropical woodland

Life on Earth

Earth may be the only planet in the universe that can support life. Our planet's oxygen and water supply are needed in order for living things to survive.

Rainforest life

There are many millions of species, or types, of animals and plants on Earth. Tropical rainforests are home to more than one half of the world's plant and animal species.

When life began

Scientists believe that life
on Earth began more
than 3.5 billion years ago.
It has been slowly evolving,
or changing, ever since then.
Remains of ancient creatures
tell us a lot about what life
was like a very long time ago.

In the sea

The oceans were the homes
of the world's first animals.
Some ocean species, such
as sea turtles, are more
than 200 million
years old.

oxygen—one of the gases in air

Earth's riches

Many of Earth's natural riches are hidden deep under the ground. Fossil fuels are found in rocks, thousands of feet below Earth's surface. They are made from the remains of ancient plants and animals.

Minerals

Rocks are made from minerals. Rare minerals, such as the diamonds and rubies in this crown, are called gems.

mineral—*a hard, natural substance*

Oil and gas

Oil and gas are fossil fuels that are pumped up from holes that are drilled into Earth's crust. They are found in places that are—or once were—under the sea.

Coal

Coal is a fossil fuel that is burned in large amounts in order to make electricity. It is dug out from deep underground mines.

Caring for Earth

Earth gives us food, water, and air to breathe. Sadly, people have not taken care of it, and many places are now polluted. Many plants and animals have died out or will soon. We must all help make Earth a cleaner place to live.

Saving forests

Trees help keep the air clean and provide shelter for many different animals. People must stop cutting down so many forests and should plant more trees.

polluted—made dirty

Recycling

We can make new things from old materials. This is called recycling. Bottles, cans, paper, plastic, and aluminum foil can all be recycled.

New energy

Scientists are developing new forms of energy that do not pollute. Many of the forces of nature, such as the wind, can be used to make electricity.

Make a volcano

Understanding eruptions

There are around 700 active volcanoes in the world today. When a volcano erupts, strong underground pressures force liquid rock up into the air. You can make your own volcano by using some simple materials. In your volcano baking soda mixes with vinegar to make carbon dioxide gas.

Using the clay, make a hollow volcano and place it on the tray. Slide the plastic bottle inside.

You will need
- Modeling clay
- Baking tray
- Small, plastic bottle with the top cut off
- Baking soda
- Funnel
- Vinegar
- Red food coloring

Half fill of the bottle with baking soda. You may need to use a funnel to do this.

Place your volcano and baking tray on top of a flat surface. You can take it outside if you prefer.

Mix the vinegar with the red food coloring. Pour the mixture into the bottle using the funnel.

Stand back and watch your volcano erupt!

Make a rain gauge

Measuring rain

There is an easy way to measure how much rain falls during a shower. Put your rain gauge out in the open. When the shower is over, open the lid and collect the rainwater in a measuring jug. Note down how much rain fell.

You will need
- Large plastic bottle
- Scissors
- Rubber bands
- Long stick
- Measuring jug
- Pen and paper

Cut a section off the plastic bottle using the scissors. You may need to ask an adult to help you do this.

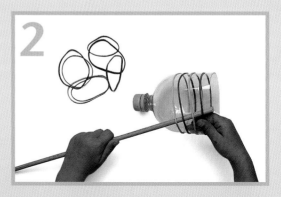

Wrap rubber bands around the bottle. Slide the stick underneath the bands and position the bottle with the screw cap facing down to catch any raindrops.

Make a windmill

Spinning sails

You cannot see the wind, but you can watch what it does. Make a windmill and see how the wind makes it move.

You will need
- 2 squares of colored paper
- Pencil and ruler
- Scissors and tape
- Thumbtack and wooden rod

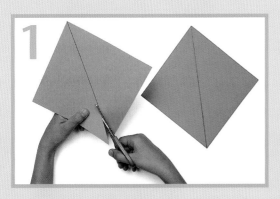

Draw a line across each paper square, from one corner to the other, using the ruler. Cut along this line to make two triangles.

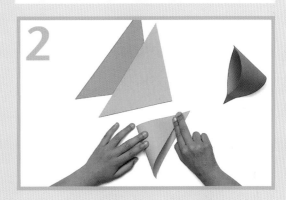

You will now have four triangles. Fold each of the triangles in half, taping the corners together.

Place the corners of the four triangles on top of each other. Ask an adult to help you attach them to the rod using a thumbtack.

Make your own forest

The place in which an animal lives is called a habitat. Everything an animal needs in order to survive can be found in its habitat—food and shelter, for example. There are many different types of animal habitats on Earth. You can make a model of a forest habitat using craft materials.

tree template to trace around

You will need
- Big shoe box
- Poster paints and paintbrush
- Pencil
- Tracing paper
- White construction paper
- Scissors
- Glue
- Modeling clay
- Plant material—leaves, grass, or twigs
- Toy forest animals

1

Paint inside your shoe box, using brown paint for the ground, green for the grass, and blue for the sky.

2

Use the template on the opposite page to trace some trees onto pieces of white construction paper. Cut out the tree shapes.

3

Paint the trees. When they are dry, use glue or clay to stick them to the bottom of the box. Scatter the plant material on the ground and arrange your animals in their new home.

Index